Big Head!

DR PETE ROWAN

For my daughter Grace

1 3 5 7 9 10 8 6 4 2

Text © Dr Pete Rowan 1998

Illustrations © John Temperton 1998

Design and Art Direction by Peter Bennett
Consultant for anatomical illustrations: Lydia Umney

First published in the United Kingdom 1998
by The Bodley Head Children's Books
Random House, 20 Vauxhall Bridge Road, London SW1V 2SA

Random House Australia (Pty) Limited
20 Alfred Street, Milsons Point, Sydney,
New South Wales 2061, Australia

Random House New Zealand Limited
18 Poland Road, Glenfield,
Auckland 10, New Zealand

Random House South Africa (Pty) Limited
Endulini, 5A Jubilee Road
Parktown 2193, South Africa

Random House UK Limited Reg. No. 954009

A CIP catalogue record for this book
is available from the British Library

ISBN 0 370 32406 4

Printed in Singapore by Tien Wah Press (Pte) Ltd

Acknowledgements
The author would like to thank his friend Dr John Pilling for his help in checking the facts in this book.
Special thanks – as usual – to Kate Petty, for being a wonderful editor.

Big Head!

DR PETE ROWAN

WITH ILLUSTRATIONS BY
JOHN TEMPERTON

THE BODLEY HEAD
LONDON

Contents

Introduction

Are you a Big Head? The straight answer is Yes! Human beings have large heads compared to total body size. And in particular it is the top part of the brain – the cerebral cortex – that is the largest part of all. What this means is that you have on your shoulders now one of the most amazing creations ever seen by the eye – itself an incredible part of your Big Head. Turn the pages of this book and you'll see all the stages of construction as, starting with a single nerve cell, a whole head is assembled. Along the way, discover some of the things that this example of the most complex living tissue on Earth can do for you: from speaking your mind and expressing your personality to more down-to-earth matters such as eating, protecting your brain and feeding and watering your body.

And the exciting thing about the brain is that the more you use it, the better it gets at the tasks you give it. Use your head with the tests and experiments in this book and you'll certainly improve your Intelligence Quota (IQ).

Other creatures have had different-sized heads and brains. The most brainless animal that ever lived was Stegasaurus (plated lizard) which roamed the United States 150 million years ago with a brain the size of a walnut. This tiny brain controlled a body that weighed 1.75 tonnes and was 9 metres long!

FACE FACTS

Your brain was assembled in a similar way to the brain in this book. Over eight months before you were born a simple tiny tube of tissue began to develop inside your mother. This was to become the brain and spinal cord. The tube became bent in some places and swollen in others, until your amazingly complex nervous system took its final shape.

USE YOUR HEAD

Could you weigh your head if you wanted? I weighed one once when I was an anatomy student at medical school. It had been cut off its body and I put it in a string bag and hung it on some scales. It had belonged to a man and it weighed about 3 kg. There are three ways you could weigh your own head. The most accurate method would be to cut it off (keeping the blood) and put the lot on a set of scales. This isn't really practical and can be exceptionally messy.

The next method would be to lie on the floor and put your head on a set of bathroom scales. This isn't very accurate because your neck muscles could not completely relax, making your head seem lighter than it really is.

The third way uses a bucket of water. Fill it to the brim, then stick your head in. Take it out when the water has overflowed. Then fill the bucket up again, carefully measuring the water needed to do this. This equals the amount of water your head displaced. One litre (1000 ml) of water weighs 1 kg (1000 grams), so if your head displaces 1500 ml of water, it weighs 1500 grams. This method assumes that your head and water are the same density. They are not exactly, but the heavier bone is offset by the lighter air-filled cavities of your sinuses, and as your brain is 85% water anyway, it is fairly accurate.

The human with the smallest-ever brain was interesting. Daniel Lyon was his name and he lived in New York about a hundred years ago. He could read and write and he worked as a night-watchman for twenty years before he died. His brain was half the weight of yours and only 180 grams more than an ape's. Amazingly, he lived a normal life. This probably means that people (like you and me) with normal-sized brains could achieve much more with them than we do. In other words, the potential of your brain is enormous.

FACE FACTS

New ways of taking pictures (PET scans – or Positron Emission Tomography) of a living brain can now enable us to see the brain actually in action. For the first time it will be possible to produce images of your brain as you do things – like reading this book and speaking about it later to your friends, so that you can literally 'see' pictures of yourself making up your mind.

The largest brain on Earth is the 9 kg one of the sperm whale. However, that is only 0.02% of the whale's weight. The human brain weighs in at about 1400 g but this is 2% of our body weight. So how big is yours? Does size matter? If you're a girl it's probable that your brain is slightly smaller than the brains of the boys in your class. This may be an interesting fact, but it doesn't mean much because brain size is not linked to intelligence.

Look at Yourself

The mind: the most elusive part of the human body

H old the opposite page up behind your head and look into a mirror for a moment.

In the other pages of this book you will find images of how your brain and head would look if you could actually see under the skin. Right now you can look in the mirror and see yourself as the world sees you. And you are looking at a real example of one of the most complex creatures ever to have roamed the Earth.

As you look into your own eyes you see much more than just a face. You are looking into, and thinking about, your mind. Abstract ideas like mind, personality, will, spirit and intellect are impossible to picture, but they make up what many people consider to be the very soul of an individual; that which, to quote the dictionary, is 'the spirit or immaterial part of a person, the part of you that survives after death'.

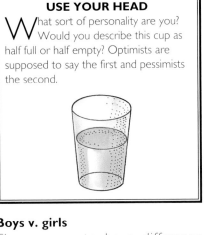

USE YOUR HEAD

W hat sort of personality are you? Would you describe this cup as half full or half empty? Optimists are supposed to say the first and pessimists the second.

Boys v. girls

There seems to be a difference between the brains of boys and girls – quite what is a mystery. Modern scans support this theory but the best attitiude is to treat everyone as an individual so that you see what a person *can* do rather than assume what they are *supposed* to do.

Einstein's brain

An attempt to preserve the brilliant mind of the physicist Albert Einstein was made after he died in 1955. His brain was removed and preserved in a bottle. Of course, the powers of his mind – its electricity and chemistry – had long since gone when the brain turned up in 1978, pickled in formaldehyde under a beer cooler in a doctor's office in Kansas.

Beauty box

What is a beautiful face? Computers have been used to try and measure loveliness mathematically. Key distances, such as eyes to nose, nose to mouth and mouth to chin, were fed into a computer and compared. There were startling similarities between many famous beauties. However, one in particular did not fit the computer's blueprint – Marilyn Monroe's eyes were too far apart and her nose was too short! Many saw this as a victory of chemistry over computing.

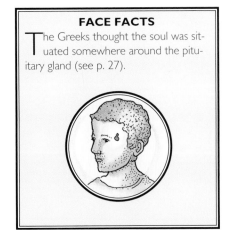

FACE FACTS

T he Greeks thought the soul was situated somewhere around the pituitary gland (see p. 27).

The Mind and Personality

Watch this space. It will help you to locate what you are looking at in the main picture.

The **eyes**, windows of the soul?

Eyebrows, can they indicate how intelligent you are?

Is your **mouth** smiley, sensuous, grim?

Do the **proportions of your face** conform to the ideals of beauty?

Does your **chin** give away your attitude?

Highway to the Head
The neck: fastest speedway in the body

Your neck is the superhighway to your head. While you are at rest, air is being sucked down into your lungs at about 10 km/h. (Give a cough and it may shoot out at up to 167 km/h!) The next time you take a drink, the fluid will travel down your gullet (oesophagus) at speeds approaching 0.7 km/h. Right now blood is rushing along arteries at nearly 3 km/h (though it is returning to your heart in veins at a more leisurely pace). But as you read this, the fastest speeds occurring anywhere in your body are along your spinal cord in your neck, where messages to and from your brain are hurtling along spinal nerves at roughly 432 km/h.

As well as your airways, gullet, blood vessels and nerves, your neck has a less visible but just as crucial transport system: the endocrine system, which is controlled by chemical messengers called hormones. The thyroid gland is a good example of one of the body's endocrine glands. The ultimate control is from your pituitary gland (see p. 27), but under its guidance your thyroid gland sends hormones into your bloodstream to affect the growth, waste disposal and energy of nearly every cell in your body.

Your neck is like a vital motorway with continual traffic moving day and night between your body and your head.

Voice box

Your larynx has three jobs.
1 It is part of the open passageway for air to enter your lungs. **2** It contains a 'trapdoor' that helps direct air and food in the right direction – to the lungs and stomach respectively. (Any mistake here and you choke). **3** It houses your vocal cords – two bands of tissue which can make noises (your voice) as air passes between them.

2 Epiglottis

3 Vocal cords

1 Trachea

USE YOUR HEAD

To locate some of the most vital structures of your neck, lie on a bed and lift your head up. The sternomastoid muscles can easily be felt as a strap down each side of your neck. Underneath them lie the carotid artery, the internal jugular vein and the vagus nerve. This nerve arises from the medulla of the brain and runs through your neck to your chest and abdomen where, amongst other organs, it supplies your heart, lungs and intestines. Through the vagus nerve your medulla (part of the brain stem) controls your heart rate, blood pressure, breathing and digestion without your having to have any conscious control over these complex functions. Next time your stomach rumbles – that's your vagus nerve at work.

All neck

Giraffes grow taller than a double-decker bus and half of this height is neck. A giraffe has an incredibly strong heart to pump blood up to the animal's head. There are also valves in the neck's blood vessels to stop the rush of blood to the head that might otherwise happen when the giraffe bends down! Like you, the giraffe has seven neck bones (cervical vertebrae) – they each just happen to be 28 cm long!

The Neck

Your neck is probably about the same length as my son Edward's (see top right), but the longest neck ever measured was 40 cm! It belonged to a woman of the Padaung tribe in Burma. It was stretched by fitting copper rings one by one to form a column.

The **carotid arteries** supply oxygenated blood to your head.

The **jugular veins** drain blood away from the head and neck and back to the heart.

The **thyroid gland** sits like a butterfly over the trachea.

The **trachea** carries air to and from the lungs during breathing.

Spinal cord

The word **oesophagus** (gullet) comes from a Greek word meaning 'carry food', which is exactly what it does – from the mouth to the stomach.

Vagus nerve *en route* to the rest of your body.

Larynx – the origin of the sound of your voice (behind thyroid cartilage).

Inside Your Head

The human head: the most complex living tissue anywhere on Earth.

Imagine that you could peel back your face. Suddenly the unique appearance on display to the rest of the world has gone, because unless you have an identical twin there is no one else in the world with a face like yours.

First remove the skin and the hair, as if the face was a mask. This would be a very bloody business because of all the arteries, veins, muscles and nerves that wind over your face.

Sitting underneath all this tissue is the bony case of the skull. Safe within its protection and watching the world through your two eyes is the brain itself. Here, beneath a spooky collection of 22 bones is the essential you.

As you read on and turn the pages of this book you will see the single basic unit of your brain – the neurone or brain cell – build up into the incredible structure that sits proudly on top of your shoulders: your **Big Head!**

FACE FACTS

Girls' faces are on average 20% smaller than boys'.

The plump cheeks on a baby's face enable it to suckle more efficiently and comfortably.

Humans rely on the face to relay subtle meanings far more than other primates do. A chimp is more likely to bark and flash the eyes than to smirk or raise an eyebrow.

Hair

Humans have much less body hair than most of the other 4,000 varieties of mammals. Nowhere is this more obvious than the face, although many men shave off this hair every day. One theory about the differences between the sexes is that it makes recognition easier at a distance. A beard, for example, indicates a man – someone you might wish to meet with, or someone to avoid if he looks fierce.

Evolution of the face

Human faces have developed with the eyes at the front for binocular vision, and the jaw low down and forward. Compare this with the more primitive 'face' of the shark which has eyes on either side of the head and a jaw slung under the head.

Brain surgery

Surgeons usually get to the brain by drilling a hole in the skull over the area they wish to operate on. We know from prehistoric skulls that this method, called trepanning, has been around for thousands of years! Other methods are through the nose or along the blood vessels in the neck.

The Skull

The skull is the most complex bony structure in the body. Most of its 22 bones are flat. All the bones apart from the lower jaw are linked tightly together by zigzag joints called sutures.

The cranium

or brain box has evolved over millions of years into a rounded structure that allows for the maximum amount of brain within the minimum amount of skull.

The eye sockets

are deep and safe containers to protect your eyes.

The 14 facial bones

provide a frame for the muscles that move your face and protect the delicate sense organs of smell and hearing.

Teeth

guard the mouth – the hole through which they will cut up and chew the food which will become you. You really are what you eat!

SKULL AND CROSSBONES

In many cultures the skull is a powerful symbol of death. A pirate used it on his flag, the Jolly Roger (probably from the French *jolie rouge*, 'pretty red' or 'bloody'), to strike terror into the hearts of his victims.

The lower jaw

is the only mobile bone in the skull. The strength of your bite is strong enough to hold the entire weight of your body.

Communications Network

Brain cells: the cells in your body with the longest life

Inside your Big Head right now there are about 100,000,000,000 living nerve cells (also known as brain cells or neurones). Each one has hundreds of connections with other nerve cells, and electrical impulses are buzzing around their circuits like balls in a super-charged pinball machine. This maze of nerve fibres will control every body cell as you work your way through *Big Head!* As you move, think, remember, sense and feel, they are there. Being special cells, they have special features. They can't store energy and need a continuous good supply of both food (glucose) and oxygen. So you must be eating and breathing to get through the book safely. Unfortunately, if nerve cells die they can't be replaced – they are lost for ever.

FACE FACTS

Nerve cells carry electrical messages in one direction only – sensory messages to the brain and motor messages out of it.

Individual nerve fibres tend to be grouped together into visible 'nerves'.

All your 'thinking' is done by electricity and chemicals!

Bird brain cells

In 1872 an Italian scientist named Camillo Golgi accidentally knocked a piece of owl's brain into a solution of silver nitrate. After several days Golgi took it out and looked at it under his microscope. He saw cells which had been stained by the silver nitrate. These were the brain's neurones. Golgi was the first person ever to see a single neurone. He won the Nobel Prize for his work.

Simple minds

The hydra is a jellyfish-like creature which lives in fresh water attached to weeds. Life is pretty dull in a pond and a hydra's days are a fairly simple business. It doesn't move much and does little more than use its tentacles to catch food which happens to drift by. Instead of a brain it has a simple nerve network. If something interesting happens in the pond, then an electrical message slowly spreads around this network. Our lives are more lively and complex than a hydra's. So humans have developed a collection of neurones which we call the brain and spinal cord.

USE YOUR HEAD

You can measure how fast nerve impulses travel through your head. Ask someone to drop a ruler between your thumb and forefinger. You must react quickly without knowing when it will be released. Measure in centimetres how much of the ruler has fallen before you catch it.

This is the sequence of events. You see the ruler move and visual messages travel down the optic nerve into your brain. The brain reacts and sends a message to your hand. Both electrical transmission (down nerves) and slower chemical transmission (at synapses) are in action here, and the whole process may be over in 0.2 seconds. The fastest nerve cells are carrying messages along their axons at an amazing 120 metres per second (432 km/h).

A Brain Cell

This is a picture of a single typical brain or nerve cell (neurone) magnified more than a thousand times. Nerve cells come in many different shapes and sizes, but they all share these similar features.

The **cell body** is the headquarters of the neurone.

Dendrites
collect incoming messages for their nerve cell.

An **axon** carries messages away from the cell body.

Synapses
are the tiny gaps between the end of one nerve cell and the beginning of the next. This is where nerve cells use chemicals to communicate messages to one another.

Nervous Reactions

The fastest type of nervous reaction

is the reflex

There are about a million motor nerves coming *down* your spinal cord from the cortex of your brain (see p. 30) at the moment. These control hand actions, like turning pages, and leg movements, like crossing your legs. They are carrying impulses as you sit reading this book. Meanwhile, information from your senses is entering the back of your spinal cord to travel *up* it and be appreciated by your brain. Information such as pain, touch and temperature (hot or cold) arrive from nerve endings in your skin. And important messages about the position of your body come from special sensors in your muscles, joints and tendons.

Inside your head there is a system of caves and tunnels shaped something like a prehistoric bird in flight. They are called ventricles. Sloshing around in these caverns right now is a pale, watery liquid called cerebrospinal fluid (CSF). About half a cupful of this fluid extends around the outside of your brain within membranes called meninges (see p. 33) and your brain floats in it. This arrangement supports the soft, jelly-like brain, which would otherwise collapse under its own weight. Cerebrospinal fluid is formed from blood by the knots of capillaries that hang from the roof of each of the four ventricles.

Renaissance discovery

Leonardo da Vinci was one of the first people to realise the real shape of the ventri-cles inside the brain. For thousands of years before, they had always been drawn as spheres. Leonardo poured hot wax into the ventricles of a dead ox to reveal the true shape of the system shown in blue on the opposite page.

Brain bypass

Reflexes are very useful emergency reactions that bypass the thinking brain to avoid potential harmful delay, for example when a ball is flying towards your face or you touch something hot. As warning sensations enter the spinal cord, signals flash straight out again to the muscles. The messages do travel to the conscious mind, but by the time they get there you have blinked or taken your hand away from the hotplate.

The Spinal Cord, Ventricles and Cerebrospinal Fluid

The spinal cord leaves your skull through a large hole and runs down as far as your lower back within your backbone. It's about 40 cm long. The 'grey matter' in the centre is mostly nerve cells. The 'white matter' outside the cells are bundles of nerve fibres going to and from your brain.

3rd ventricle

Lateral ventricles

4th ventricle
This is the smallest ventricle.

Central canal
This canal containing cerebrospinal fluid connects with the system of hollow ventricles in the head and runs down the centre of the spinal cord.

Spinal cord
Thirty-one pairs of spinal nerves branch out from the spinal cord to serve the torso, arms and legs.

**Cerebrospinal fluid
(shown in blue)**
This fluid that protects your brain is formed in your blood. Floating in it, the brain is effectively almost weightless.

Your Subconscious

The brain stem: the only part of the the nervous system without which life is impossible

As you read this, just ten per cent of your brain tissue stands between you and sudden death. The brain stem is the only part of the nervous system to have this power. What makes it even more remarkable is that most of the time you're not conscious of what it is doing.

Here in the brain stem lie the rigidly programmed clusters of nerve cells necessary for survival. While you are reading this book they are subconsciously controlling your heart rate, blood pressure and breathing, as well as the transport of your last meal through your intestines. From here, signals can flash out like thunderbolts to spark off coughing, sneezing, hiccupping or vomiting.

THE IMPORTANCE OF DREAMS

Dreams are obviously important. In an experiment carried out several years ago a cat deprived of the dreaming phase of sleep died after twenty days. One theory suggests that we use dreams as a time for discarding unnecessary information, rather than storing it in the long-term memory. This theory has the unlikely support of the hedgehog-like echidna, which has a huge brain for its size. This egg-laying marsupial does not have REM sleep (so perhaps does not dream) and may need its large brain to store information rather than dream it away.

Dream on

Last night and again tonight and probably every night for the rest of your life a small cluster of 30,000 blue cells in the part of the brain stem called the pons will begin to fire. This is where your dreams are born. During the dreaming phase of sleep your cortex builds up these impulses from the pons into a kaleidoscope of the adventures that we call a dream. This seems to be a time when your brain sorts out or tidies up various memories, thoughts and experiences.

Scientists can monitor dreams because they occur during the rapid eye movement (REM) phase of sleep, and these movements under the closed eyelids are easily visible.

INTERPRETING DREAMS

The Austrian psychoanalyst, Sigmund Freud, said that dreams were the 'royal road to the unconscious' and wrote a book about interpreting them. He believed a dream in which you are pulled from water symbolises birth – as in leaving the fluid in which all babies float before birth. Here are some other common interpretations of dreams:

Falling – worry about failure at school or in exams.

Being naked – feeling over-sensitive or vulnerable.

Flying – confidence.

Reptile brain

In reptiles and fish the brain stem forms the main part of the brain. The lack of emotion and conscious thought that originates from this area means that you won't be greeted with a smile from the tortoise or a wag of the tail from the gold-fish when you come home from school.

The Brain Stem

The brain stem connects the spinal cord to the rest of the brain. The three parts of the brain stem, the pons, the midbrain and the medulla, are each about 2.5 cm long.

The **midbrain** coordinates head and eye movement. It contains the highest number of motor neurones in the central nervous system.

The **pyramids** are huge bundles of fibres that make a landmark on the medulla. They carry messages for skilled controlled movement from the cerebral cortex to the body's muscles.

The **pons** is mainly made up of tracts of nerve fibres linking the cerebral cortex with the spinal cord and the cerebellum (see p. 25). It controls sleep and dreams.

The **medulla** This is the vomiting centre of your brain.

Brain Filter

The reticular formation: the supreme gatekeeper to your conscious mind

Interesting as these words are, if an elephant suddenly charged towards you now I bet you would very quickly notice it. As the ground rumbled, the room vibrated with trumpeting sounds, and two large tusks flashed by your throat, you would become aware that the largest living land animal was breathing down your neck. But the arrival of the elephant would be only a fraction of about 100 million pieces of information being fed into your nervous system at that moment. Information from your eyes, ears, tongue, nose and from the touch receptors in your skin would still be arriving at the gateway of your nervous system. What's taking your mind off all of these and allowing you to notice the elephant?

The answer is that 99% of all the information coming to you is filtered out by a piece of brain stem not much bigger than your little finger. Your reticular formation (RF) is continually sorting and sifting incoming messages and allows only what might be necessary or important – maybe the sudden smell of smoke – to be 'appreciated' by the higher parts of your brain. Without the RF you would literally go crazy.

Homework in front of the TV

The RF is kept active by all its incoming information and in turn it keeps your cerebral cortex 'awake'. Parents are often baffled when their children insist that they can work with the TV on. But the children might be right! It is possible that the increased work for the RF in filtering out all the extra distractions keeps the cerebral cortex alert.

The reticular formation

The RF enables the top tennis player to concentrate only on hitting the ball – shutting out all other distracting information coming into the brain. Players often find they go through a big game without hearing the shouts of the crowd or feeling the pain of an injury until the match is over.

USE YOUR HEAD

Take your watch off. Prove to yourself that you can feel the watch and then put it on again. Your skin will register all the sensations as you do this. Maybe the watch is cold or feels rough or smooth. Then put your arm behind your back. After a few moments your RF begins to filter out the messages from the skin around the watch and it becomes quite difficult to tell if you have a watch on or not!

FACE FACTS

The RF can also register the absence of sensations the brain has become accustomed to. People living by a railway get used to the noise of trains running while they are asleep, but can be woken up if a familiar train fails to run by their house!

The Reticular Formation

This is an intricate connection of nerve cells extending through the core of the brain stem.

The exceptional feature of the **reticular formation** is the large numbers of connections it makes with other parts of the brain and spinal cord. The 10 dark brown clusters shown in the picture are clusters of RF nerve cells. Impulses from these literally keep the rest of the brain awake and make this the arousal centre of the nervous system.

Drugs

The effects of drugs on the brain are clearly seen in spiders and the webs they weave.

1 Unfinished web of a laid-back spider on marijuana.

2 Drunk spider falls asleep on the job.

3 Shaky web of an anxious spider on a high dose of caffeine (coffee).

'MIND-EXPANDING' DRUGS

The drug LSD (lysergic acid diethylamide) reduces the action of the RF. Users may suddenly find increased awareness of sensual perceptions that might otherwise have been filtered out, such as sound and colours.

LSD has very curious effects on animals. Siamese fighting fish float nose up, goats do silly walks and spiders spin fantastic but useless webs. One elephant dropped dead after being given LSD. It's best avoided.

Balance and Coordination

The cerebellum: the part of the brain with the most nerve cell connections

S top reading these words for a moment and bend your head back to look up. Then ask yourself this question, 'Do I know where my feet are?' You do of course, even though you can't see them, just as, if you decided to take a few steps, you wouldn't have to look down and check their position. The reason you can do these actions without thinking about them – and much more complicated things, like riding a bike or running down stairs – is because of a computer-like part of your brain called the cerebellum ('little brain'), which functions rather like the autopilot of a plane. It's continually receiving information about the position of your body from your eyes, ears and the nerve endings near your muscles and joints. It processes all this so that your body can move around in a smooth and well balanced way without your thinking brain – the cerebral cortex – being involved.

Try 'thinking' about running down stairs . . . It's much easier to let the cerebellum work out the movements on its own for this!

YUK!

The brain can become confused if it receives conflicting information about the position of your body. If your eyes are telling it one thing about the horizon and your inner ear another – when you are on a boat, for example – it can't reconcile the two and you might feel seasick.

Cat walk

A cat has a large cerebellum for its size. This is partly what is responsible for its typically graceful movements and usually enables it to land on its feet however it falls.

Evolution

Australopithecus, an ancestor of modern man who lived one and a half to two million years ago, had a very well developed cerebellum. The space for it can be seen in fossil skulls. This is evidence that he or she had good, coordinated hand movements and could use tools such as stone axes. By comparison, the chimpanzee has a small cerebellum and does not use hand tools or facial expressions as we do.

Heavy metal

The first visible signs of a cerebellum that isn't working properly are what you would expect – a reeling, staggering walk, slurred speech and shaky hands.

The metal mercury can damage the nervous system and in particular it targets the cerebellum. In many countries mercury is used to dress seed before it is sown to protect it from fungi as the crop grows. There was a large-scale epidemic of cerebellar disease in Iraq a few years ago when bread was made from mercury-dressed seed rather than from the crop which the seed should have produced.

The Cerebellum

The cerebellum makes up about 11% of your brain. Folds in its surface keep 85% of this hidden from view. In cross section it looks rather like a small cauliflower (see p. 41).

THE MOST COMPLEX BRAIN CELLS
PURKINJE CELLS

The nerve cells of the cerebellum – Purkinje cells – are amongst the most complex brain cells you have. They are tree-shaped and the 'branches', or dendrites, may make contact through synapses with 100,000 other nerve fibres – more connections than any others in the brain.

Cerebellum

Like the rest of the brain the cerebellum has a left side and a right side. If you feel your head at the back, around where the hairline ends, these two computers are just under the surface.

Body Clock

The hypothalamus: the most accurate clock in your body

Ticking away inside your head right now is your inbuilt biological clock – a living timepiece controlled by your hypothalamus. It follows roughly the solar 24-hour cycle of day and night, and takes its cues from the light levels coming from your eyes. Very few parts of your body escape its influence. This 'clock' is a group of cells within the hypothalamus no bigger than a few grains of sand!

It's 10 am as I write these words. By this time of day most of us are completely awake and brain activity is at its peak. Unless your biological clock has been upset – perhaps by jet lag – you can check your watch or a clock and see where you are in today's time cycle (right).

12 noon Appetite is stimulated for food (energy).

10 am Fully alert. Kidneys on full power and forming urine.

2 pm Many people feel slightly sleepy after lunch. This could be the effect of digesting the food.

8 - 10 pm Depending on your age your body is ready to 'clock off' and rest for 8 - 10 hours.

6 pm Dusk falls (the exact time depends on the time of year). A hormone is secreted which tends to cause sleepiness.

3 am Body temperature falls. Heart slows. Urine production falls. Episodes of REM sleep and dreams occur. Brain activity reduced.

8 am Heart rate and blood pressure go up as you begin to move around. Draw the curtains and the light of the rising sun confirms with your brain's clock that it really is time to begin an active day.

6 am Body temperature rises. Chemicals prepare the body for activity. Energy stores are mobilised.

The Hypothalamus, Thalamus and Pituitary

The hypothalamus is located just under the egg-shaped thalamus and at 4 g (the size of four peas) makes up 0.5% of the total brain weight. However, for its size it has no rivals in its great influence over your body. The pituitary gland helps control your endocrine glands which in turn control your hormones. The thalamus works with the 'thinking' brain (the cerebral cortex) to organise information from your senses.

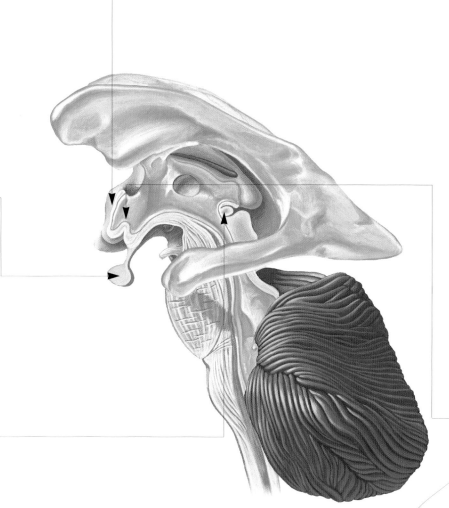

Thalamus
The thalamus has only a basic appreciation of sensations, such as whether something is pleasant or unpleasant. It is here that receptors interact with drugs to relieve pain.

Pituitary gland
Hormones secreted by this gland include growth hormone. People who are extra tall or short may have some problem with their pituitary gland.

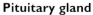

Pineal gland
This is sometimes called a 'third eye' because although it is deep inside your brain it receives information about light levels from your eyes and is involved in setting your body's clock.

Hypothalamus
This regulates your autonomic system. It influences many different body activities such as blood pressure, heart rate, breathing, body temperature, appetites for food, drink and sex as well as movement of food in the gut. It is also the centre for your emotional responses (see limbic system, p. 29), making you ready to run when you are scared, for example.

Emotions

The limbic system: the most emotional area of your body

The limbic system is the mysterious bubbling cauldron in which all your pleasures, pains and memories are brewed – your 'emotional brain'. At the moment it is impossible for me to tell what's going on in that part of your brain, because events in the limbic system depend on personal things, like your past life, your memories and what has influenced you.

Most of the time your limbic system balances your emotions. However, sometimes the limbic system may be almost overwhelmed by emotion and, if this spills over to the brain areas that deal with movement and language, you may become paralysed by fear or left speechless. As the limbic system is so closely linked with areas that deal with heart rate and digestion, like the hypothalamus, it's not surprising that emotion can also play havoc with these in the form of high blood pressure and stomach ulcers. The ultimate blow that the limbic system can deliver to its own body is death. Terrible grief and emotion can even cause the heart to stop.

Your emotional brain distinguishes between at least two sorts of memory. **Fact** memory holds names, dates, facts and faces. These can be very easy to forget! Once in the long-term memory they are usually filed along with an experience. So if you meet friends while swimming on holiday you'll remember them in the pool in their swimsuits. **Skill** memory holds activities such as riding a bike. Unlike facts, these are very difficult to forget. Skills like tying your shoelaces are almost impossible to 'unlearn'.

> ### USE YOUR HEAD
> (Don't try this!)
>
> A Spaniard called José Delgado implanted an electrode into the limbic system of an aggressive bull. He then stood in front of the animal with his transmitter. The bull charged as soon as it saw him, but when Delgado fired the transmitter the bull stopped immediately and became very friendly!
>
>

Nostalgia

As memory is handled in the limbic system, it's also no surprise to discover links between memory and emotions. And because the sensation of smell enters the brain through the limbic system, smell is the most emotive of all the senses. It has the power to trigger powerful memories. I've only to return to my old school and smell the floor polish to remember exactly what it was like to do exams, be told off, and look forward to the summer holidays. There will be smells that do the same for you!

> ### FACE FACTS
>
> Déjà vu means 'already seen' in French, and it's that feeling of something having already happened. Maybe you visit a place you've never been to and really feel you've seen it before. This could be because for some reason your brain has stored your first impressions as if they were recalled memory.

Short-term and long-term memory

Short-term memory (STM) lasts about 30 seconds – just about long enough to dial a phone number before you forget it. Use STM often and it will be converted to long-term memory (LTM). LTM must involve permanent changes in the brain, as many memories last a lifetime. Repeating facts as well as understanding them improves the transfer of STM to LTM.

The Limbic System

The limbic system is a wishbone-shaped arrangement of nerve tissue wrapped around the top of your brain stem. It links the lower parts of the brain with the higher reasoning centres of the cerebral cortex. Your sense of smell – unlike your senses of sight, taste, hearing or touch – is plugged directly into it.

The **fornix** is a bundle of fibres carrying messages of memory and emotion from the hippocampus.

The **mamillary bodies** are two pea-like structures that relay smell impulses.

The **hippocampus** is essential for learning. It converts short-term memory into long-term memory.

The **amygdala** is where fear learned from experience is stored. A rat with its amygdala removed has been known to lose all fear of cats!

Thinking, Learning and Speaking

The cerebral cortex: the most human part of the brain

It is from your cerebral cortex that you think, see, hear, imagine, but most humanly of all where you speak your mind! (And maybe later decide to change it, too.) Please quietly read the next sentence out aloud. You are now using the most brilliant technical achievement of the brain. (You can stop now.) What you just did sets you apart from all the other animals on Earth. Imagine where TV, radio, books, school work and conversation with friends would be without language. All of us remember and think in words.

BRAIN QUIZ

What's wrong with this paragraph? Possibly it's just slightly unusual. You should try now and find out what's going through my mind as I pick out my words with caution. Don't look through it too quickly – study it analytically and in a painstaking way. With a bit of luck – and your thinking brain's vast capacity for brilliant thought – you should find what is so unfamiliar about it. Tax your mind if you don't crack it at first and try again. Don't miss anything. It isn't that difficult!   **Solution**

Brain exercises

If you solved the puzzle above you did it using the reasoning powers of your cerebral cortex (just I cm under the hair on your head!)

faCT. Iq STaNDS FoR INTeLLiGENCe quoTa. ONe DeFiNiTioN oF iT iS BeiNG aBLe To THiNK LaTeRaLLY. liKe ReaLiSiNG WHaT'S GoiNG oN NoW. tHaT iS THaT THe uSuaL WaY oF uSiNG CaPiTaLS aND LoWeR CaSe LeTTeRS HaS BeeN ReVeRSeD. (EXCePT FoR VoWeLS.)

By working your brain like this you will improve it. Experiments have shown that learning to play with toys (and doing quizzes) actually thickens the cerebral cortex as the ten thousand million nerve cells make more connections with one another. It's happening now! It works best in childhood, so the younger you learn something, the better. Any adult who tries to take up the piano will tell you that!

Now you can try out your thinking brain. **1** Look around at any object close by you. **2** Now say the name out loud. **3** Your brain is hearing the word as you say it. **4** Finally, the most interesting part of the experiment: think up something to say about the object. For example, if your object is a pencil you might think, 'that's something I can write with'.

Speaking sentences is a very much more complicated event than the simple outline above. Your teacher asks you a sudden question in class. You must choose the correct words, organise some grammar, and then physically speak the words – all in a split second.

1 Seeing 'words'   **2** Speaking words   **3** Hearing words   **4** Generating ideas about words

PET (Positron Emission Tomography) scans

are able to show the brain in action. The bright colours in the four scans above indicate where your brain is active as you use language.

Practice makes Perfect

These scans show the difference between a boy playing a computer game for the first time (left – lots of activity) and after two months of practice (right – very little activity).

Areas of the cerebral cortex (right)

1 Movement	**5** Vision
2 Basic movement	**6** Hearing
3 Sensation	**7** Speech
4 Visual association	**8** Behaviour

The Cerebral Cortex

The two cerebral hemispheres cover the brain stem like a mushroom covers its stalk. The outer layer, called the cortex, looks wrinkled because of its many folds. This grey matter is like the bark that covers a tree and is only about 2-4 mm thick. Its folds increase the total area by three times what it would be if it were smooth. The grey matter packed into your skull would roughly cover the surface of your pillow if you could iron it out!

Your **dominant cerebral hemisphere (1)** if you are right-handed is the left one. It mostly controls reading, writing, reasoning and arithmetic. It's connected to your other hemisphere, which deals more with the emotional and creative areas of your life, by a thick bundle of nerves called the **corpus callosum (2)**. This links the two hemispheres and enables them to share things like learning and memory, attention and awareness. The dominant hemisphere keeps the whole show running smoothly.

The **basal ganglia (3)** are large collections of nerve cell bodies that (with the cerebellum) keep body movements smooth and coordinated.

MAN TAN

In the spring of 1861 a man who for 21 years had been able to say only the word 'tan' died. He understood when spoken to and could communicate by using hand signals and facial expressions. After his death an area the size of a hen's egg was found to be missing from his left cerebral hemisphere. This was a scientific milestone, as language – at least part of it – had been traced to one particular area of the brain. Much of our information about the workings of the brain has come from the study of damaged brains like Tan's.

Temporal lobe

Frontal lobes

Protecting and Feeding the Brain

The most sensitive part of the brain:

the meninges

The bony plates that form your skull will protect your brain from everyday knocks, but the layers of the meninges that line the inside of the cranium provide a second and less obvious line of defence. The brain floats within this vital liquid cushion (see p. 18) which, although only amounting to about half a cupful (150 ml) in total, is still able to be an important shock-absorber against blows to the head.

Right now your heart is pumping out about five litres of blood every minute. And about 20% of this is sent to the head up the four main arteries. Your brain is taking more oxygen out of this blood at the moment than any other part of your body. It uses 20% of all the oxygen your lungs breathe in. The brain runs on this oxygen and on glucose (sugar). It needs nothing else. Every day this 'computer', which is 85% water, uses no more than about the same amount of energy as a 10-watt light bulb.

FACE FACTS

Head wounds often look worse than they actually are. This is because the scalp has the richest supply of blood anywhere on the surface of your body and cuts bleed especially heavily.

Meningitis

People get meningitis when germs get into the meninges. It's serious because these germs can easily spread from here to the brain. Some of the main symptoms are headache, fever, vomiting, lethargy and a stiff neck. It needs urgent treatment. The diagnosis is usually made by passing a thin steel needle between the bones of the spine into the cerebrospinal fluid and finding the germ.

FIRST AID

Brain cells are not able to store energy like other body cells. This is why they die in minutes if their blood and oxygen is cut off. You can learn how to deal with this emergency in First Aid classes. The basis of the procedure called resuscitation is as easy as ABC.

A Airways. Keep open so air gets to the patient's lungs.
B Breathing. If the patient isn't, you must do it for them.
C Circulation. If blood isn't moving around the body you must give heart massage.

Ever seen a rabbit in glasses?

Carrots contain carotene which helps make Vitamin A in your body. Vitamin A is necessary to see in the dark. This is the basis for the old wives' tale about carrots making you see better at night!

USE YOUR HEAD

Your scalp moves very easily over your skull. This is because the fibrous tissue in the layer just above the bone is very loosely attached. You can test this yourself by massaging your own scalp. It's interesting to think that the thoughts you are having about this matter are coming from only a few millimetres below your massaging fingers.

The Meninges and Blood Vessels

The brain is covered by three layers of tissue called the meninges. The outer layer is tough and leathery. There is CSF between the middle and inner meninges. Blood vessels run over the brain's cerebral cortex.

Dura mater
The toughest outer layer of the meninges.

Pia mater
The delicate inner layer of the meninges.

The **arteries** (red) carry blood to the the brain.

The **arachnoid mater** is the spiderweb - like middle layer of the meninges.

The **veins** (blue) carry blood away from the brain and back to the heart.

The **scalp** is made up of five layers of tissue. The tissue under the skin has some fat but it is so firmly bound down with fibrous tissue that even the fattest people do not get 'fat' on the top of their heads! There just isn't enough space.

Head Lines

The most specialized lines of communication anywhere in the body: the cranial nerves

At the top of your body, as you may have noticed, is your big head. It's large in comparison to other animal heads because of its big brain. Humans need brains this size to cope with all the information coming in and out of an upright body, and to do all the things that can be done with two hands – free now to be used for skilled tasks rather than for walking on all fours. Right now, twelve pairs of cranial nerves are carrying information *to* your brain and commands *from* it. These pass out of the base of your skull through holes called the foramina. The complex receptors at the other ends of some of these nerves – the eyes, the tongue, the nose and the ears – are found nowhere else in the body!

Head movement

Head movement is a very important thing to have, in particular for directing vison. Watching a tennis match is a simple example.

Your bony skull is carried on the first cervical vertebra (atlas), like the world on the shoulders of Atlas in Greek mythology. Smooth joints between it and your skull allow you to nod your head as you say Yes. Subtle movements are taking place at this joint now as your eyes move and you read *down* the page.

Looking at the skull from the side it seems to be perched rather precariously on the smaller bones of the vertebral column. However, powerful muscles – mainly at the back of your neck – keep it safe and steady on your shoulders. Under the atlas bone is the second cervical vertebra (axis). This has a peg at the front which sticks up and 'locks' into the atlas above. This pivot joint enables you to shake your head and signal No. You are moving it slightly (and your eyes too) as you read *across* the page. These movements are performed by the muscles around the neck (p. 12-13).

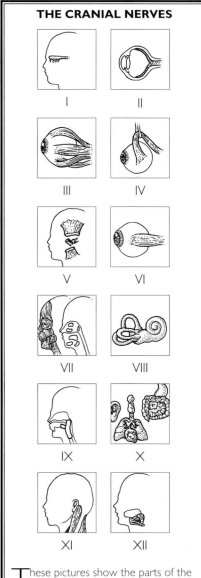

THE CRANIAL NERVES

I   II
III   IV
V   VI
VII   VIII
IX   X
XI   XII

These pictures show the parts of the body served by each of the 12 pairs of cranial nerves.

Four eyes – no brain

The most poisonous creature in the sea is the box jellyfish (or sea wasp) found along the North Australian coast and around South-East Asia. Each of its deadly body's four sides has an eye complete with lens and cornea. These eyes can certainly 'see' because the jellyfish can move away from anything it finds threatening. But no one knows what they are connected to. Your cranial nerves can be traced as they run from organs like your eyes into your brain. But where in the transparent body of this eerie monster is the brain which receives the messages from those four eyes?

The Cranial Nerves

Traditionally the twelve pairs of cranial nerves are numbered using Roman numerals. The vagus (vagus means wandering) is the only one of the twelve to leave the head and neck.

I The **olfactory nerve** of smell.

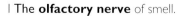

II The **optic nerve** from the retina of the eye.

III The **oculomotor nerve** controls four of the six muscles that move each eye.

IV The **trochlear nerve** controls another muscle that moves the eye.

V The **trigeminal nerve** carries messages of sensation from the face, nose and mouth.

VI The **abducens nerve** controls the other muscle that moves the eye.

VII The **facial nerve** controls the muscles of facial expression and the smallest muscle in the body – the stapedius – inside the ear. It also carries the sensation of taste from the front two-thirds of the tongue as well as controlling four of the six salivary glands and the muscles of the pharynx.

VIII The **vestibulocochlear nerve.** The vestibular part deals with balance, and the cochlear part with hearing.

IX The **glossopharyngeal nerve** carries taste sensation from the back one-third of the tongue. It supplies the parotid salivary glands and some of the swallowing muscles as well as sensations from the back of the mouth and pharynx.

X The **vagus nerve** 'wanders' down the body to control the heartbeat, breathing muscles, gut mobility and some of the liver and kidney.

XI The **accessory nerve** controls some of the neck muscles.

XII The **hypoglossal nerve** controls the muscles that move the tongue.

The arrows point to only one nerve in each pair.

Vision

The head's greatest source of information:

the eye

Your eyes are obviously open as you read this, but one of the best ways to appreciate the most complex visual system of any animal is to close your eyes. Do it now for a few seconds. . .

Most of us have an uneasy, vulnerable and slightly lonely feeling when deprived of sight. Even after a few seconds there is great relief when you can open your eyes and rejoin the colourful visual world.

Down each optic nerve of your two eyes come thousands of millions of pieces of fresh information every second. Ten million shades of light and seven million of colour contribute to a human's richest sense. Seventy-five per cent of all the information that your brain will gather today will come from your eyes. Sometimes your eyes are likened to a TV camera – but there is a profound difference. Vision is in your brain – not in your eye. The information coming into your head is assembled into what you 'see' by the visual cortex (see opposite p. 31). It is here that electrical signs from the retina are given real meaning. Damage to the cortex can blind you even though your eyes might be in perfectly good working order.

Eyes bigger than its stomach

The muscles that you use to roll your eyes are used by toads for a quite different job. Toads have no teeth in their lower jaw. This is unfortunate when you like to eat insects. So what the toad does is to lower its eye muscles through a kind of trapdoor in their sockets and hold the insects while its upper teeth chew them. The only disadvantage is that the toad can't see when it eats, but maybe you'd close your eyes if someone put a plate of beetles and blue-bottles down in front of you!

Tea for two

Different areas of your visual cortex handle different aspects of what you see. A lady called Gisela Leibold damaged the area where her eyes 'saw' and handled movement of images. One big problem for her was that she couldn't pour a cup of tea without over-filling the cup. She couldn't see it filling up – just lots of 'frozen' images of a teapot, a stream of tea from the spout, a cup with more and more tea in it, but no movement! She solved the problem by marking the inside of her cup near the top. When the line disappeared she stopped pouring.

The Eye

Two eyes at the front of your head have adapted to provide you with a precise and focused view of the world around. Less efficient than an owl's at night, not as keen as a hawk's in the day, not as wide-ranging as a deer's in the forest, they can nevertheless move quickly from a book to a distant star, see colours, adapt to changes in light, estimate distances and direction, and bring two images into one for perfect 3-D vision.

The **retina** contains light-sensitive cells — the rods and cones.

Rods are the 125 million cells sensitive to the brightness of light.

Cones are the 7 million cells which detect colour. There are three types and each is sensitive to either red, blue or green.

The **lens** focuses light onto the retina.

The **pupil** is the hole through which light enters the eye. In the mirror yours look like dark spots in the centre of each eye.

The **iris** is coloured either blue, green, grey or brown, and can make the pupil bigger or smaller depending on the amount of light.

The **optic nerve** carries light messages to the brain.

The **cornea** is transparent and covers the front of the eye.

The **sclera** is the tough coat that covers the eyeball. It is the 'white' of the eye.

Hearing

The (middle) ear: the site where more is accomplished per square millimetre than anywhere else in your body

Listen to what you can hear at the moment. Maybe the TV is on or a bird is singing. Perhaps someone is talking. Whatever sound is being produced around you, some of its energy is travelling through the air to your ear. So, like the ripple from a stone thrown into a pond, these waves of sound are reaching you now.

As they do, the part of your ear that you can see in a mirror (the pinna) is collecting them and channelling them down the canal to your eardrum. It's vibrating now – slowly for low sounds and faster for the higher ones. These vibrations pass across the three smallest bones in your body. This is the 'bridge of bones' to your inner ear. Here lies the greatest wonder of the ear. This is where you can pick out one voice at a noisy party or hear from a low hum right up to a high-pitched wailing shriek. Here the sound waves (vibrations) are turned into nerve impulses that travel to your brain up the eighth cranial nerve (see p. 35). When they reach your auditory cortex – well, you are listening to the result now.

Spirit level

The first sense organ ever developed on Earth may have been a simple balance organ in a jellyfish. You can still see these if you look closely at the base of a tentacle (don't get stung). When a sudden wave sweeps across the creature and tilts this spirit level, the jellyfish can react and right itself. Your inner ear has a similar balance mechanism. On the top of the cochlea are three semicircular tubes set at right angles to one another. They contain a liquid which moves when you move your head. Messages from this enable your brain to tell you what position you are in. So you may not be able to sting, but you do have one thing in common with the most poisonous creature in the sea (see p. 34).

'Ear, 'ear

The first airborne communications were probably between insects. Many insects have ears on places other than their heads. Butterflies have them at the base of their wings, mosquitoes on their antenna and some grasshoppers below their knees! This may seem funny, but for these creatures hearing can be the difference between life and death. The praying mantis has a special ear where you have a belly button just to listen out for the hunting cry of the bat that likes to eat it!

Noises in the dark

A normal ear can tell the difference between about 40,000 different sounds. You have two ears, just as you have two eyes, so they can work together to locate noise and find things in a 3-D world. Your ears are much better at telling sounds coming from the left or the right than from high up or low down. A barn owl, on the other hand, has one ear higher than the other so that it can locate sounds more accurately.

The Ear

The ear can be divided into three parts: the outer ear (pinna and auditory canal); the middle ear (the cavity inside the skull bone which contains the hammer, anvil and stapes); and the inner ear, which also deals with balance.

The three small bones in the middle ear are named after their shapes. They carry the sound from the **eardrum** to the **auditory nerve.**

Eardrum

Hammer bone

Anvil bone

The Stirrup bone (stapes)

The **stapedius** is the smallest muscle in your body. It can move the stapes bone and deaden loud sounds which would otherwise damage your hearing.

Cochlea

Pinna

Eardrum

Semi-circular canals

Auditory nerve

Ear canal

Breathing, Smelling and Eating

The nose: the only visible part of your respiratory system

One thing is certain, right now your head is inhaling and exhaling air. If you spent the whole of today resting you would take about twelve breaths every minute, and each one of those breaths would take in about 400 ml of air. In a day this means you would breathe a total of about 7,000 litres. Some of this air is now entering the upper part of the airways of your head (from your nose, to your sinuses and your pharynx) and swirling round these cavities. It's being cleaned, warmed and moistened before it travels in a few seconds from now down to your lungs. By the time it reaches the inside of your chest it is as warm and damp as a tropical jungle. Today the small glands lining the inside of your nose will produce an amazing one litre of fluid to trap and kill the dust, germs and other debris that you will breathe in with the 7,000 litres of air. You won't notice much of this as tiny brushes (cilia) gently waft and sweep all this fluid back down your throat where it is eventually swallowed and destroyed by stomach acid.

Smelling

The olfactory (smelling) nerves enter the brain via the limbic system at a lower level than nerves for the other senses. Smell is the chief sense for many animals. But although smell is a primitive sense it is also a very complicated one. The eye recognises three primary colours and the tongue four basic tastes, but no one has ever managed to simplify smell in this way. One theory has seven primary smells: floral, musky, camphorous, peppermint, ethereal, pungent and putrid.

> **FACE FACTS**
>
> The air is warmed in your nose by blood running in large veins just under the surface of the lining of the nasal cavity. Because of their size and large numbers and the position they are in, nose bleeds are quite common and may be quite heavy.

> **USE YOUR HEAD**
>
> Smell is the one sense that gets bored very easily. Put a small dab of a smelly substance like perfume on your upper lip just below your nose. For a short while you'll appreciate the smell, but quite quickly your brain will block it out and you'll soon stop noticing it. This can be very useful, and is the reason why sewer workers can still enjoy their lunch while at work.

The hole through which nearly all of your body has travelled: your mouth

Over 99% of the body now reading this book has travelled through your mouth! Think back to the main meal you had yesterday. Since you ate it it has been broken down (digestion) in your bowel, moved across the bowel wall (absorption), and now is becoming part of you (assimilation). Fate has cast food and your head together for ever. Your head has your mouth on its face. This is where that meal, like all the food you'll ever eat, entered your body. That food set off your senses of smell and taste so that your head realised what was in store. Your head began digestion by chewing and chopping the food up. The food carried this process on by triggering the six salivary glands around your mouth. These added the first chemicals (enzymes) to break the food down. Then your head moved (swallowed) the food in mouthfuls down your oesophagus and into your stomach.

> **The tongue**
> The tongue is the only muscle in your body that is loose at one end!

The Nose and Mouth

Tongue

Teeth

Oesophagus

Olfactory nerve

Chewing muscles

Salivary glands

Making Faces

The most intricate signalling equipment in the world: the facial muscles

Touch your face. Messages about skin texture and body temperature flash to your brain, but what you can't tell from touch is the image you show to the rest of the world. How do you think your face looks now? While you are reading it's probably quite expressionless, but if a friend were to walk in, the hundred or so muscles under your skin would start their small subtle contractions to signal your mood and your feelings about the other person. The signals to move these muscles of facial expression are coming from your brain's motor cortex, and are easy to control. However, there is also a lot of subconscious input from the lower brain as the messages travel down to your face, and these are not easy to control. This is what makes good acting very difficult.

Facial expressions

Faces all over the world show six basic emotions. These are anger, disgust, fear, happiness, sadness and surprise. Even those blind from birth have these. This supports the idea that these feelings are not learned, but programmed into your brain's 'hard disk' before you were born.

Happiness

Sadness

Anger

Surprise

Fear

Disgust

The Facial Muscles

These are the muscles of facial expression shown after the head has been skinned. These muscles signal feelings, open and shut the eyes and mouth, and move the lips and cheeks when you speak. They are unusual since many are connected to skin or other muscles rather than bone. They tend to be arranged in a circular fashion around the orifices of the face.

The **frontalis** raises the eyebrows in surprise.

The **corrugator supercilii** (hidden by the frontalis) pulls the eyebrows together to frown.

The **orbicularis oculi** 'screws' up the eyes in intense light (and is responsible for the 'crows' feet of old age).

The **buccinator** (hidden by the masseter muscle) is the main muscle of the cheek. It's used for eating and playing the trumpet!

The **zygomaticus** raises the corners of the mouth when you smile.

The **depressor labii inferioris** pulls the lower lip down to pout.

The **levator labii superioris** opens lips and flares nostrils.

The **depressor anguli oris** pulls the mouth down to grimace.

The **orbicularis oris** is the kissing muscle.